Your Amazing Itty Bitty™ Keep Your Children Safe Book

15 Key Steps to Educating and Protecting Children from Online Predators, Trafficking, and Sextortion

Lynda J. Bergh Herring

Published by Itty Bitty™ Publishing
A subsidiary of S & P Productions, Inc.

Copyright © 2024 Lynda J. Bergh Herring

All rights reserved. No part of this book may be reproduced or transmitted in any form or by any means, electronic or mechanical, including photocopying, recording, or by any information storage and retrieval system, without written permission of the publisher, except for the inclusion of brief quotations in a review.

Printed in the United States of America

Itty Bitty Publishing
311 Main Street, Suite D
El Segundo, CA 90245
(310) 640-8885

ISBN: 978-1-959964-97-1

Disclaimer:

This book, *Your Amazing Itty Bitty™ Keep Your Children Safe Book: 15 Key Steps to Educating and Protecting Children from Online Predators, Trafficking, and Sextortion,* is for educational purposes only and is not a substitute for professional advice when talking with your child (children) about the dangers of cyber-crime.

Your Amazing Itty Bitty™ Keep Your Children Safe Book

15 Key Steps to Educating and Protecting Children from Online Predators, Trafficking, and Sextortion

Human trafficking involves using force, fraud, or coercion to obtain some form of labor or commercial sex act. Every year millions of men, women, and children are trafficked worldwide. This includes Sextortion, where individuals are blackmailed into giving money or sexual favors to someone threatening to reveal evidence of their sexual activity. The vast majority of human trafficking and sextortion begins online.

In her book, Your Amazing Itty Bitty ™ Keep Your Children Safe Book, Lynda Bergh Herring will educate you on protecting your children from online predators, trafficking and sextortion.

She offers guidance on:

- Talking to your children about social media dangers
- Monitoring your children's online activity
- Recognizing online predators
- Tips to keep your children safe
- And so much more

If you or anyone you know is concerned about the safety of your children, pick up a copy of this must-read Itty Bitty™ book today!

I dedicate this book to my mentor, Nancy Poss Hatchl, without whom I would never have discovered the world of private investigation, and also to the survivors of trafficking and sextortion who work tirelessly to recover from their trauma, and help others before, during, and after the experiences they endured.

Stop by our Itty Bitty™ website to find interesting information regarding Human Trafficking and Sextortion.

www.IttyBittyPublishing.com

Or visit Lynda J. Bergh Herring at

https://www.keepyourchildrensafe.com

Table of Contents

Introduction
Step 1. Human Trafficking and Sextortion: It's in Your Neighborhood
Step 2. Sextortion is Happening in Your Home
Step 3. Who Is at Risk?
Step 4. My Child Would Never Do That
Step 5. That Will Never Happen to Me
Step 6. I've Talked to My Kids About the Dangers of Social Media
Step 7. Online Enticement
Step 8. Create a Social Media Contract
Step 9. Monitor Your Children's Online Activity
Step 10. How to Recognize an Online Predator
Step 11. Signs Your Child Is Being Groomed or Exploited
Step 12. Would You Recognize Trafficking or Sextortion if You Saw It?
Step 13. If You See Something, Say Something
Step 14. If Your Child is the Victim of Online Exploitation or Sextortion
Step 15. Top Tips to Keep Your Children Safe

Introduction

Human trafficking involves the use of force, fraud, or coercion to obtain some form of labor or commercial sex act. Every year millions of men, women, and children are trafficked worldwide.

Sextortion is the practice of extorting money or sexual favors from someone by threatening to reveal evidence of their sexual activity. Sextortion is a greatly increasing daily threat to children, with many victims committing suicide because they do not know what else to do.

The vast majority of human trafficking and sextortion begins online. In this book, you will learn not only how to recognize online predators and signs your children may exhibit if they're being groomed or trafficked, but also how to monitor their activities, and what to do if your children fall victim to either of these crimes.

Step 1
Human Trafficking and Sextortion: It's in Your Neighborhood

Traffickers are not who you think they are.

1. Ninety percent of trafficking begins online.
2. Trafficking is not limited to labor or commercial sex.
3. The white panel van is now the internet.
4. The United States is one of the top countries for trafficking.
5. Trafficking is the fastest-growing criminal industry in the world, a $150B industry second only to the drug trade.

Victims are not who you think they are.

1. Not all victims are taken to or from another country.
2. There is no socioeconomic status or restriction.
3. Victims of trafficking are not just girls; boys are trafficked too.

More About Trafficking and Sextortion

It is not unusual for teenage girls or boys to run away for only a day or two and then return in the process of trafficking.

- They live at home, go to school, and spend the afternoon with friends, but are still being trafficked.
- Classmates are trained to recruit fellow classmates as young as elementary school.
- Statistics show that a child who runs away will be recruited to sell drugs or be trafficked.

Trafficking is not new; it's even mentioned in the Bible.

- Your manicurist could be trafficked, your massage therapist, gardener, or even the housekeeper next door.
- Traffickers can be anybody: your neighbor, your child's teacher, a police officer, minister, or coach, not just the creepy guy living in his mom's basement.

Step 2
Sextortion is Happening in Your Home

Sextortion starts innocently, but often ends tragically.

1. It starts with a social media friend request, most often someone posing as a teenage girl.
2. The victim is groomed, flirted with, love bombed, and then a request is made for a nude or provocative photo or video showing the victim's face.
3. Once the photo is received by the perpetrator, the extortion process begins.

The perpetrator threatens to send the illicit photo or video to the victim's friends, family, school, etc.

1. The perpetrator will instantly distribute the photo or video to their circle of fellow predators on the dark net.
2. Money is most often demanded from boys, and additional photos or videos from girls.
3. Once the photo or video is sent, there is no way to ever get it back.

More About Sextortion

Sextortion can have tragic consequences.

- Sextortion can lead to the victim committing suicide, often within a few hours of their initial contact with the predator.
- In some cases, sextortion goes on for years without the victim ever telling anyone.
- Sextortion and sextortion-related suicides can occur overnight while mom and dad are sleeping with no idea what's happening in their child's bedroom.

Sextortion is increasing everywhere all over the world, according to news and law enforcement reports to www.missingkids.org.

- The increase is attributed to 5G mobile networks, allowing internet access to literally every person in the world.
- Sextortion rings often originate in the Ivory Coast, the Philippines, and Morocco, but an ever-increasing number of perpetrators are being identified and arrested in the United States.

Step 3
Who Is at Risk?

Victims of trafficking and sextortion can be of any race, gender, or nationality.

1. The average age a child is first trafficked is 12.
2. It is estimated that one in five trafficking victims are children.
3. Youth in or from foster care are most at risk for trafficking, along with runaway and homeless teens and young adults.
4. Recent immigrants and those suffering from mental health issues or substance abuse are also at risk.
5. In the vast majority of sex trafficking cases, the victim has a history of child sexual abuse.

Additional risk factors that could apply to any preteen, teen, or young adult include:

1. The desire to make money
2. The desire to be loved, accepted, admired, or included

More About Who Is at Risk

Not all trafficked or sextortion victims are immigrants or come from broken homes.

- Sextortion rings target preteens and teens involved in organized sports and youth organizations, as well as college groups such as sororities and fraternities.
- Sextortion perpetrators have begun demanding access to the victim's parent's business, or banking information seeking larger value payouts.
- According to medical experts, young males are particularly vulnerable to sextortion-related scams because their brains are still developing.

Sextortion can also be perpetrated in the form of revenge porn.

- Revenge porn is the distribution of previously shared intimate images by a former partner, often to embarrass or punish the victim.
- Victims can suffer guilt, anger, paranoia, depression, or even suicide.

Step 4
My Child Would Never Do That

When asked about their child's social media interaction with strangers, parents nearly always believe their kids would never do that.

1. Children and young adults do not recognize online "stranger danger" as they would in a public place.
2. Since the interactions are online, kids do not consider what they're doing to be real.
3. The majority of kids' initial sexual interaction takes place in the virtual world, often with someone they only know online.

Stranger danger is everywhere.

1. Nearly every app and gaming platform has a chat feature, which predators typically use to contact potential victims.
2. Your child should frequently be reminded to never accept a friend or connection request from a stranger.

More About My Child Would Never Do That

Primary risk factors that lead to sextortion or enticement include:

- A child lying about their age to access platforms where they can communicate with older individuals.
- Being contacted by an individual online or offering to provide sexually explicit images to the individual in exchange for financial compensation, alcohol or drugs, gifts, etc.
- Sending sexually explicit photos or videos of oneself to another individual.

According to the National Center for Missing and Exploited Children:

- Forty percent of kids 13 to 17 say it is "normal" to share nude photos.
- One in five kids say it's okay to share a nude photo as long as it's sent using an app that doesn't save it, such as Snapchat. They don't think about the other party screenshotting the post before it disappears.

Step 5
That Will Never Happen to Me

Children, especially teenagers, believe they are invincible.

1. Teens do not believe sex trafficking and sextortion occur, especially in their own "safe" neighborhood.
2. Teens believe they can spot or outsmart a predator. They cannot.
3. Traffickers and sextorters are master manipulators who know what to say and do to victimize children.

Predators often start as friends or intimate partners.

1. At first, the perpetrator showers the teen with gifts and compliments, promising to give them everything their parents won't, including taking them places.
2. Before long, the victim finds themselves in a situation they can't get out of, often involving sex with their so-called love's friend.

Then they are forced to earn money, which they never get to keep.

More About That Will Never Happen to Me

Kids don't have the wherewithal or maturity to protect themselves from predators.

- Many cases of sex trafficking are never reported due to fear, intimidation, or because the victim is unable to do so.
- Some victims are afraid to report for fear they will be arrested for sharing their own photos or taking part in illegal sexual activity, even though they were coerced to participate.

Sextortion victims are afraid to report what is happening to them.

- They are embarrassed and ashamed.
- Victims are often afraid to report sextortion, fearing they will get in trouble for sending child pornography. They don't realize they are victims who were manipulated by a predator. It is not the child's fault!
- AI-created sextortion is a growing threat to everyone, children and adults. Kids who fall victim to AI sextortion feel trapped, as they have no feasible way to convince others the images are not really them.

Step 6
I've Talked to My Kids About the Dangers of Social Media

Telling your kids to be careful is not enough.

1. Social media is a dangerous place for kids and adults.
2. Romance scams, phishing attacks, child exploitation, and trafficking are all rampant online.
3. Many adults have no idea how to handle those issues; kids definitely do not.

Have you warned your kids about sharing personal information online?

1. A simple Google search of your name reveals a lot of information, including your name and age, family members' names and ages, addresses, telephone numbers, places of employment, schools, and more.
2. Predators rarely have to conduct a Google search because your child is already sharing the above information with them.

The entire family is placed at risk.

More About I've Talked to My Kids About the Dangers of Social Media

Talk to your children about what they're sharing online.

- Your kids need to protect themselves as well as their younger siblings.
- Remind them that when they take part in a video chat, the person they chat with can see them and whoever is behind them, such as a younger sibling.

Backgrounds in photos and metadata can expose your children to predators. Using privacy settings and turning off location settings are great offensive moves to protect your children.

- There are documented cases of stalkers finding victims by zooming in on reflections on their sunglasses in photos.
- Younger siblings of sextortion and trafficking victims have been targeted after being seen in the background during video chats.
- Predators have identified schools, vehicles, home addresses, and locations where kids play sports by studying photos posted online.

Step 7
Online Enticement

Online enticement is defined as someone communicating with a child via the internet with intent to exploit them.

1. Every parent should be worried about online enticement.
2. If your child has access to the internet, predators have access to your child.
3. Most online enticement involves sexual intent.

Online enticement often leads to meeting in person, which can have dire consequences.

1. Most children are enticed online via conversations with an adult on social media sites, messenger apps, and gaming site chat rooms.
2. Most offenders of online enticement are male, and typically ten or more years older than the child.
3. In-person meetups with offenders can lead to kidnapping, rape, trafficking, and even murder.

More About Online Enticement

Important facts about online enticement include the following.

- Most children who leave home due to online enticement first speak with adults online before their missing incident.
- Few children make noticeable attempts to conceal who they talk to.
- Most missing children connected to online enticement, are 15 years old or less.
- Offenders are typically 20- to 29-years-old, but tend to be at least ten years older than the child.
- Missing children enticed online often travel great distances before returning home or being located.
- More than a third are recovered in a different state, and many are located in a neighboring county.
- Offenders in online enticement cases are overwhelmingly male.

Step 8
Create a Social Media Contract

Before your child is ever given a phone or any device with internet access, have them sign a contract, including the points below.

1. They agree to discuss and share every app with parent(s), how they are used, including passwords and PINs.
2. They agree to never share a photo, video, or livestream anything that could cause harm or embarrassment.
3. They agree never to meet with someone they have met online.
4. They agree that if they're threatened in any way, they will tell you, a trusted adult such as a teacher, pastor, or grandparent, and report the incident to the appropriate authorities.

Report inappropriate content.

1. All apps and online platforms have simple procedures for reporting inappropriate content.
2. Report any child sex abuse material to law enforcement, NCMEC (National Center for Missing and Exploited Children), and the Department of Homeland Security.

More About Social Media Contracts

Effective communication is key. Be sure your kids have someone who believes in them to talk to. They need to tell someone immediately if:

- They're approached or contacted by anyone inappropriately online
- Someone makes them feel bad, sad, scared or confused

Although it may not always feel like it, kids need to know that there are people who believe in them and are willing to help.

Step 9
Monitor Your Children's Online Activity

The best way to keep your children safe from online predators is to monitor their internet use.

1. Limit the amount of computer and mobile phone use.
2. Children should not sleep with their phone or devices nearby; ideally in a separate room. NCMEC reports 67% of children sleep with their electronics.
3. Be familiar with the apps and platforms they use. Most parents only know the top two. Most kids use a dozen or more apps; favorites vary according to popular trends.
4. Do you know how many friends and followers they have? Do you know who they follow?

Privacy settings are essential on social media.

1. Friends, followers, school, birthdate, address, family members, and photos should all be set to private.
2. For birthday messages, list only month, day, and no birth year on their profile.
3. Location settings should be turned off.

More About Monitoring Your Children's Online Activity

Learn how to find hidden apps on your children's phones, because kids are "evil geniuses" when it comes to hiding things.

- A simple Google search will lead you to instructions on finding hidden apps on Android and iPhone devices.
- There are techniques available to conduct forensic searches of electronic devices, including apps, text and chat messages, videos, etc.
- A commonly-used app favored by predators to store illicit photos and videos is Keepsafe, which you may find hidden behind the calculator application on their devices. If you find it, demand the PIN, or better yet delete the app.

If they complain or balk about monitoring their access, remind them that the devices belong to you, the person who signed the contract who also pays the bill. You are *lending* your devices to them. Monitoring is not a violation of their privacy, but rather a way to protect them.

Step 10
How To Recognize an Online Predator

Even though predators are master manipulators, recognizing them is not that difficult. Here are some obvious signs the person contacting you or your child is a predator.

1. The first question they ask is, "How old are you?"
2. Their profile is new, with few friends or posts.
3. There are no or few connections or mutual friends.
4. The profile photo is an avatar.

The predator will invite your child to move from their original communication app to another "more private" messenger or chat location.

1. This is like being kidnapped on the street and taken to a second location. Don't do it!
2. Once that move is made, there is danger ahead for your child.
3. It takes only eight minutes for a predator to gain the trust of your child.

More About How to Recognize an Online Predator

It takes only 10 minutes for a predator to request a "more interesting" or illicit photo, and only 50 minutes for them to ask to meet in person.

- The predator will ask your child many personal questions, including whether or not they get along with you.
- Predators love kids who are not getting along with mom and dad, are confused about their sexuality, or are having trouble in school.
- The predator will tell your child not to tell anyone about them, preferring to remain a "special, secret" friend.
- The new predator will pepper your child with questions but divulge nothing about him or herself. Nothing.
- The new friend will request additional "more interesting" photos from your child.

Step 11
Signs Your Child Is Being Groomed or Exploited

If your child is exhibiting the following behavior, he or she may be in danger.

1. Spending more time on the phone or other devices
2. Drop in grades
3. Trouble sleeping
4. Truancy, missing school
5. Hiding things suddenly when you appear, especially activity on their devices
6. Becoming nervous when the phone rings
7. Spending more time alone in their room
8. New online friends but no details
9. Talk about moving or running away
10. Job offers too good to be true
11. Signs of a fantasy relationship
12. Expensive gifts from an unknown source
13. A second or new device you did not purchase
14. Sudden new phone or device

More About Grooming and Exploitation

Predators often create "fantasy relationships" during the grooming process. Ask your child about their new love interest.

- Do they know where the new boyfriend/girlfriend lives, works, and goes to school? Do they know their hobbies, favorite movies, or the music they like?
- They can't answer questions about the predator because nothing has been divulged—nothing at all.

You may notice personality and behavioral changes as well.

- An introverted child suddenly becomes extroverted or language changes, including slang.
- You notice changes in wardrobe, hair, makeup, or personal hygiene.

Step 12
Would You Recognize Trafficking or Sextortion if You Saw It?

Child trafficking victims display at least some of the following signs.

1. They appear malnourished, anorexic, or bulimic.
2. They avoid eye contact, social interactions, and law enforcement.
3. Responses are rehearsed because traffickers tell them exactly what to say and not say.
4. They withhold names or personal information.
5. They don't have IDs or personal possessions, not even a phone—or conversely, they may have two phones.
6. They're confused; they may not know where they are and why.
7. Victims have unexplained bruises or other injuries. Cutting is common among victims.
8. They are with someone constantly who is literally controlling and physically attached to the victim in public.

More About Recognizing Trafficking or Sextortion

Trafficking victims are sold and advertised in many places.

- In chat rooms or via messenger
- Prostitution or massage parlor review sites
- On the streets
- At large events and private parties
- In hotels and motels
- In brothels, massage parlors, apartments, and private residences
- Via webcam sex

Many children are trafficked and advertised in online sex ads. Profiles of kids for sale can easily be found on social media.

- Apps such as Tinder, Grindr, TikTok, Facebook, Instagram, and Wizz are the current preferences.
- Apps and platforms change frequently. For an updated list, visit the following: https://www.keepyourchildrensafe.com/dangerousapps.

Step 13
If You See Something, Say Something

Many trafficking and sextortion crimes go unreported. That needs to change.

1. Trafficking cases are investigated by local law enforcement, along with the Federal Bureau of Investigation and the Department of Homeland Security.
2. Sextortion is investigated by the Department of Homeland Security Cyber Crimes Center, but only if reported.

Many trafficking victims have been rescued from tips to law enforcement.

1. Calls to 911 have been received from airline employees/passengers, restaurant workers, retail employees and patrons, and the general public.
2. Law enforcement far prefers false alarms to recovering a child who was kidnapped, raped, trafficked, or murdered.

More About If You See Something, Say Something

For your safety and your family's, do not try to take action against a trafficker or sextortionist on your own.

To report suspected human trafficking, contact:

National Human Trafficking Hotline
1-888-373-7888

Department of Homeland Security
https://www.dhs.gov/see-something-say-something

When you submit your tip, DHS will request the following:

- Who or what you saw
- When you saw it
- Where it occurred
- Description of the situation

National Center for Missing and Exploited Children Hotline: 1-800-848-5678

Step 14
If Your Child Is a Victim of Online Exploitation or Sextortion

If your child is a victim of sextortion or social media exploitation, take the steps outlined below.

1. Do NOT delete the photos; save screenshots and videos.
2. Do NOT share photos or videos with anyone other than law enforcement.
3. Do NOT interact with the perpetrator. Screenshot the online communication, then block their accounts.
4. Take the phone/device and your child to local law enforcement and ask for the cybercrimes unit or report the incident to Homeland Security or NCMEC.

This is a chance for your child to be a hero.

1. There is no way out of blackmail or extortion until it is reported.
2. By reporting the crime, your child sets a good example for younger siblings and friends.
3. Most importantly, be sure your child knows they have not changed in your eyes. You still love and believe in them.

More About Victims of Online Exploitation or Sextortion

Another side of sextortion involves extortion of family members.

- The FBI reports that predators may contact parents and friends of sextortion victims who committed suicide to get money from them. Never pay a predator.
- Predators use AI to create explicit images of children to extort them or parents for cash. Again, never pay them.

If your child has illicit photos or videos on the internet, *Take It Down* is a new platform developed by NCMEC to help them report their consensual imagery to have it taken offline.

https://takeitdown.ncmec.org/

The minor is not required to upload or share the images. The app works with participating online platforms only. NCMEC is working to add more participating apps.

Step 15
Top Tips to Keep Your Children Safe

Open communication is extremely important.

1. Encourage your children to come to you with anything and everything, especially if something makes them uncomfortable or scared.
2. No topic is off limits, and there will be no repercussions for talking to you.
3. When your children make a mistake, you will be there to help them through it.

Monitor your children's internet activity.

1. Routinely review your child's devices. Everything! This requires knowing their passwords and PINs. This is protection for them, not a violation of their privacy.
2. All electronics should be kept outside your child's bedroom at night. No excuses!
3. Keep your children away from online games and apps, especially chat rooms, where 500,000 predators are lying in wait at any given time.

More Top Tips

Interacting with predators leads to dangerous situations. Educate yourself and your children.

- Online strangers can be more dangerous than strangers on the street. Do not interact with strangers online. What happens online is real.
- If a new online connection asks your age, do not answer. If they ask you to change platforms or apps, refuse. That's like being kidnapped!
- Everything you send into cyberspace stays there forever, no matter how much you pay.
- Never ever meet someone in person who you have only met online. Never!

Be vigilant for changes in your child's personality and behavior.

- If you see changes, ask them what's happening in their life.
- If you see what appears to be trafficking or sextortion, report it!

Be sure your children always know you believe in them, no matter what!

You've finished. Before you go …

Post/share that you finished this book.

Please star rate this book.

Reviews are solid gold to writers. Please take a few minutes to give us some itty bitty feedback.

ABOUT THE AUTHOR

Lynda J. Bergh Herring aspired to be a ballerina when she grew up (and trained to be one), but life had other plans. She began working in the private investigation industry in 1982 and was quickly assigned her first missing-child case. The circumstances were heart-wrenching, involving a 10-year-old girl kidnapped and trafficked by her uncle. The case ignited her desire to work protecting children.

She obtained her California private investigator license in 1996 and conducts many private investigations for attorneys, corporations, small business owners, and private parties. Over the years she has worked tirelessly against child trafficking, and more recently sextortion, which includes locating and rescuing children, educating parents, teachers, faith-based leaders, public safety officials, and children about staying safe from predators, both online and in the real world.

To learn more about Lynda, her investigations, workshops, and speaking engagements, visit the following:

https://www.ljbinvestigations.com/ or
www.keepyourchildrensafe.com

If you enjoyed this Itty Bitty™ book
you might also like…

- **Your Amazing Itty Bitty Communicating With Your Teenager Book ~ Christine Alisa**

- **Your Amazing Itty Bitty Video Gaming Addiction Book ~ Sean Bryan**

- **Your Amazing Itty Bitty Personal Data Protection Book ~ Karen Worstel**

Or any of the many Amazing Itty Bitty™ books available online at www.ittybittypublishing.com

www.ingramcontent.com/pod-product-compliance
Lightning Source LLC
Chambersburg PA
CBHW071313060426
42444CB00034B/2540